In the Year1942

by

Kerry Butters.

In the Year 1942.

Millennium:	2nd millennium
Centuries:	19th century – **20th century** – 21st century
Decades:	1910s 1920s 1930s – **1940s** – 1950s 1960s 1970s
Years:	1939 1940 1941 – **1942** – 1943 1944 1945

1942 (MCMXLII) was a common year starting on Thursday (dominical letter D) of the Gregorian calendar, the 1942nd year of the Common Era (CE) and *Anno Domini* (AD) designations, the 942nd year of the 2nd millennium, the 42nd year of the 20th century, and the 3rd year of the 1940s decade.

Contents

Events

Map of Europe at the height of German control in 1942, Britain remaining the only country in Western Europe held by Allied forces

January

- January 1 – WWII:
  - The Declaration by United Nations is signed by China, the UK, the USA, and the USSR in which they agree "not to make any separate peace with the Axis powers".
  - United States and Philippines troops fight the Battle of Bataan against Japanese forces.
- January 2 – WWII: Japanese warplanes bomb Manila, Philippines

- January 7 – WWII: Operation Typhoon, the German attempt to take Moscow, ends in failure.
- January 7 – WWII: The siege of the Bataan Peninsula begins.
- January 11 – WWII:
    - Dutch East Indies campaign: Japan declares war on the Netherlands and invades the Dutch East Indies.
    - Malayan Campaign: The Japanese capture Kuala Lumpur, the capital of the Federated Malay States.
- January 13
    - Sikorsky R-4 first flies, in the United States; it will become the first mass-produced helicopter.
    - Heinkel test pilot Helmut Schenk becomes the first person to escape from a stricken aircraft with an ejection seat.
- January 16 – American film actress Carole Lombard and her mother are among all 22 aboard TWA Flight 3 killed when the Douglas DC-3 plane crashes into Potosi Mountain near Las Vegas while she is returning from a tour to promote the sale of war bonds.
- January 19 – WWII:
    - Japanese forces invade Burma.
    - Establishment of United States VIII Bomber Command, later to become the Eighth Air Force, in Savannah, Georgia.
- January 20 – The Holocaust: Nazis at the Wannsee Conference in Berlin decide that the "Final Solution (*Endlösung*) to the Jewish problem" is relocation, and later extermination.
- January 21 – WWII: Erwin Rommel launches his new offensive in Cyrenaica.
- January 23 – WWII: The Battle of Rabaul begins.
- January 25 – WWII: Thailand declares war on the United States and United Kingdom.
- January 26 – WWII: The first American forces arrive in Europe, landing in Northern Ireland.
- January 31 – WWII: Malayan Campaign: The last organized Allied forces leave British Malaya, ending the 54-day campaign, and the Johor–Singapore Causeway is severed.

February

- February – C. S. Lewis's *The Screwtape Letters* first published in book format in England.
- February 1 – WWII: The Command staff of the Eighth Air Force reaches England.
- February 3 – WWII: Rommel suspends his offensive in Cyrenaica.
- February 7 – United States Maritime Commission fleet operations transferred to the War Shipping Administration (lasting until September 1, 1946).
- February 8
    - António Óscar Carmona is elected president of Portugal.
    - WWII: Top United States military leaders hold their first formal meeting to discuss American military strategy in the war.
    - Daylight saving time goes into effect in the United States.
- February 9 – The ocean liner SS *Normandie* catches fire while being converted into the troopship USS *Lafayette* (AP-53) for WWII at pier 88 in New York City: she capsizes early the following morning.
- February 11 – Operation Cerberus: A flotilla of Kriegsmarine ships dash from Brest through the English Channel to northern ports; the British fail to sink any of them.
- February 15 – WWII: Singapore surrenders to Japanese forces.
- February 18 – WWII: More than 200 American sailors die in Newfoundland when the USS *Truxtun* runs aground near Chambers Cove and the USS *Pollux* runs aground at Lawn Point.
- February 19 – WWII:
    - Japanese warplanes bomb Darwin, Australia.
    - A returning Japanese fighter plane crashes on Melville Island (Australia) and its pilot, Hajime Toyoshima, becomes the first Japanese captured on Australian soil when indigenous resident Matthias Ulungura takes him prisoner.
    - United States President Franklin D. Roosevelt signs Executive Order 9066 allowing the United States military to

define areas as exclusionary zones. These zones affect the Japanese on the West Coast, and Germans and Italians primarily on the East Coast.

- February 19-23 – WWII: Battle of Sittang Bridge – British forces retreat to the Sittaung River.
- February 20 – Lieutenant Edward O'Hare becomes America's first U.S. Navy WWII flying ace.
- February 22 – General George Marshall transmits a direct order to General MacArthur in President Roosevelt's name, ordering MacArthur himself to turn over command of the Philippines to a subordinate and report to Australia to assume command of the large American force being built up there. The orders are worded to allow MacArthur to choose the exact moment of his departure; for various reasons, he will not leave until March 12 (Eastern Date).
- February 23 – The Japanese submarine *I-17* fires 17 high-explosive shells toward an oil refinery near Santa Barbara, California, causing little damage.
- February 24
  - *Struma* disaster: MV *Struma*, carrying Jewish refugees from Axis-allied Romania to British-administered Palestine, is torpedoed and sunk by the Soviet submarine *Shch-213*, killing about 791 men, women and children, with only one survivor.
  - Propaganda: The Voice of America begins broadcasting.
- February 25 – Battle of Los Angeles: Over 1,400 AA shells are fired at an unidentified, slow-moving object in the skies over Los Angeles. The appearance of the object triggers an immediate wartime blackout over most of Southern California, with thousands of air raid wardens being deployed throughout the city. In total there are 6 deaths. Despite the several-hour barrage no planes are downed.
- February 26
  - The worst coal dust explosion to date, in Honkeiko, China, claims 1,549 lives.

- The 14th Academy Awards ceremony is held in Los Angeles; *How Green Was My Valley* wins Best Picture.
- February 27 – WWII: Battle of the Java Sea: An allied (ABDA) task force of 14 vessels under Dutch command, trying to stem a Japanese invasion of the Dutch East Indies, is defeated by a 19 vessel Japanese task force in the Java Sea; 2.300 sailors die, including the commander, admiral Karel Doorman; Japanese attain naval hegemony in East-Asia

March

- March – Construction begins on the Badger Army Ammunition Plant, the largest in the United States during WWII.
- March 9 – WWII: Executive order 9082 (February 28, 1942) comes into effect reorganizing the United States Army into three major commands: Army Ground Forces, Army Air Forces, and Services of Supply, later redesignated Army Service Forces, with Henry H. Arnold as Commanding General of the United States Army Air Forces.
- March 12 – WWII: U.S. General Douglas MacArthur, his family, and key members of his staff are evacuated by PT boat, under cover of darkness, from Corregidor in the Philippines. Command of U.S. forces in the Philippines passes to Major General Jonathan M. Wainwright.
- March 16 – WWII: New Zealand and Australia declare war on Thailand.
- March 17 – The Holocaust: the Nazi German Bełżec extermination camp opens in occupied Poland about 1 km south of the railroad station at Bełżec in the Lublin district of the General Government. At least 434,508 people are killed here up to December 1942.
- March 18 – Franklin D. Roosevelt, President of the United States, signs Executive Order 9102, creating the War Relocation Authority (WRA), which becomes responsible for the internment of Americans of Japanese and, to a lesser extent, German and Italian descent, many of them legal citizens.

- March 20 – WWII: After being forced to flee the Philippines, U.S. General Douglas MacArthur announces (in Terowie, South Australia), "I came through and I shall return."
- March 23 – WWII: The Germans burn down the Ukrainian village of Yelino (Koriukivka Raion), killing 296 civilians.
- March 24 – The evacuation of Polish nationals from the Soviet Union begins. It is conducted in two phases: until 5 April; and between 10 and 30 August 1942, by sea from Krasnovodsk to Pahlavi (Anzali), and (to a lesser extent) overland from Ashkabad to Mashhad. In all, 115,000 people are evacuated, 37,000 of them civilians, 18,000 children (7% of the number of Polish citizens originally exiled to the Soviet Union).
- March 28 – WWII: St Nazaire Raid (Operation Chariot) – British Commandos raid Saint-Nazaire on the coast of Western France to put its dockyard facilities out of action.

April

Spring 1942: the Nazi German extermination camp Treblinka II opens in occupied Poland near the village of Treblinka

- April – The Holocaust: the Nazi German extermination camp Sobibór opens in occupied Poland on the outskirts of the town of Sobibór. Between April 1942 and October 1943, at least 160,000 people are killed here.
- Spring – The Holocaust: the Nazi German extermination camp Treblinka II opens in occupied Poland near the village of

Treblinka. Between July 23, 1942 and October 1943, around 850,000 people are killed here, more than 800,000 of whom are Jews.

- April 3 – WWII: Japanese forces begin an all-out assault on the United States and Filipino troops on the Bataan Peninsula.
- April 5 – WWII: Easter Sunday Raid – Aircraft of the Japanese Navy attack Colombo in Ceylon (Sri Lanka). Royal Navy cruisers HMS *Cornwall* and HMS *Dorsetshire* are sunk southwest of the island.
- April 9 – WWII:
  - The Bataan Peninsula falls and the Bataan Death March begins.
  - The Japanese Navy launches an air raid on Trincomalee in Ceylon (Sri Lanka); the Royal Navy aircraft carrier HMS *Hermes* (95) and Royal Australian Navy destroyer HMAS *Vampire* are sunk off the country's East Coast.
- April 13 – The United States Federal Communications Commission's minimum programming time required of TV stations is cut from 15 hours to 4 hours a week during the war.
- April 14 – WWII: The submarine HMS *Upholder* is sunk.
- April 14 – WWII: The German submarine *U-85* is sunk by USS *Roper*.
- April 15 – WWII: Award of the George Cross to Malta: King George VI awards the George Cross to the island of Malta to mark the Siege of Malta, saying, "To honour her brave people I award the George Cross to the Island Fortress of Malta, to bear witness to a heroism and a devotion that will long be famous in history" (from January 1 to July 24, there is only one 24-hour period during which no bombs fall on this tiny island).
- April 17 – WWII: Henri Giraud the French commander captured in 1940, escapes from Königstein Fortress.
- April 18 – WWII: Tokyo, Japan, is attacked by the Doolittle Raid, a small force of B-25 Mitchell bomber aircraft commanded by then-Lieutenant Colonel James "Jimmy" Doolittle.
- April 23

- WWII: Exeter becomes the first historic English city bombed as part of the Baedeker Blitz in retaliation for the British bombing of Lübeck.
- Exeter-born William Temple enthroned as Archbishop of Canterbury.
- April 25 – The Princess Elizabeth registers for war service in the U.K.
- April 26 – WWII: The Reichstag meets for the last time, dissolving itself and proclaiming Adolf Hitler the "Supreme Judge of the German People", granting him the power of life and death over every German citizen.
- April 27 – WWII: A national plebiscite is held in Canada on the issue of conscription.
- April 27 – The Jewish Star of David is required wearing for all Jews in the Netherlands and Belgium; Jews in other Nazi-controlled countries have already been wearing it.
- April 29 – WWII: An explosion at a chemical factory in Tessenderlo, Belgium leaves 200 dead and 1,000 injured.

May

- May – Operation Pluto: The plan to construct oil pipelines under the English Channel between England and France is tested in the River Medway.
- May 5 – WWII – Operation Ironclad: British forces invade the French colony of Madagascar.
- May 7 – WWII: On Corregidor, the last American and Filipino forces in the Philippines surrender to the Japanese under command of 2Lt. Robert L. Obourn (92nd Coastal Artillery Corps Battalion, G Battery) from Fort Mills.
- May 8 – WWII: The Battle of the Kerch Peninsula: The German 11th Army begins Operation *Trappenjagd* (Bustard Hunt) and destroys the bridgehead of the three Soviet Armies (44th, 47th, and 51st) defending the Kerch Peninsula, in the eastern part of the Crimea.

- May 8 – WWII: The Battle of the Coral Sea (first battle in naval history where 2 enemy fleets fight without seeing each other's fleets) ends in an Allied victory.
- May 8 – WWII: The Battle of the Kerch Peninsula: German and Romanian forces launches Unternehmen Trappenjagd (Operation Busted Hunt) aiming at defeating the Soviet Crimean Front defending the Kerch Peninsula. The battle ends in Axis victory. Part of the Eastern Front.
- May 8/May 9 – WWII: At night, gunners of the Ceylon Garrison Artillery on Horsburgh Island in the Cocos Islands mutiny. The mutiny is crushed and three executed (the only British Commonwealth soldiers to be executed for mutiny during the Second World War).
- May 12 – WWII – Second Battle of Kharkov: In the eastern Ukraine, the Soviet Army initiates a major offensive. During the battle the Soviets capture the city of Kharkov from the German Army, only to be encircled and destroyed.
- May 12 – WWII: The Japanese minelayer *Okinoshima* is sunk by the American submarine USS *S-42*.
- May 14 – Aaron Copland's *Lincoln Portrait* is performed for the first time by the Cincinnati Symphony Orchestra.
- May 15 – WWII: In the United States, a bill creating the Women's Auxiliary Army Corps (WAAC) is signed into law.
- May 20 – The first African-American seamen are taken into the United States Navy.
- May 21 – WWII: Mexico declares war against Nazi Germany after the sinking of the Mexican tanker *Faja de Oro* by German submarine *U-160* off Key West.
- May 26 – WWII – Battle of Bir Hakeim: The Free French and British troops slow the German advance in North Africa.
- May 26 – WWII: Anglo-Soviet Treaty of 1942 to help establish military and political alliance between the USSR and the British Empire is signed in London by foreign Secretary Anthony Eden and by Soviet foreign minister Vyacheslav Molotov.

- May 27 – WWII – Operation Anthropoid: Czech paratroopers attempt to assassinate Reinhard Heydrich in Prague.
- May 30–31 – WWII: Bombing of Cologne – British RAF Bomber Command's "Operation Millennium", its first 1,000 bomber raid, with associated fires make 13,000 families homeless and kills around 475 people, mostly civilians; 3,330 non-residential buildings are totally destroyed.
- May 31–June 1 – WWII: Attack on Sydney Harbour: Japanese midget submarines infiltrate Sydney Harbour in Australia in an attempt to attack Allied warships.

June

June 4: The Japanese aircraft carrier, *Hiryū* under attack by US aircraft at the Battle of Midway

- June 1
  - WWII: Mexico declares war on Germany, Italy and Japan.
  - The Grand Coulee Dam is finished on the Columbia River.
- June 4 – WWII: Reinhard Heydrich succumbs to wounds sustained on May 27 from Czechoslovakian paratroopers acting in Operation Anthropoid.
- June 5 – The United States declares war on Bulgaria, Hungary & Romania.
- June 4–June 7 – WWII: The Battle of Midway: The Japanese naval advance in the Pacific is halted.

- June 7 – WWII: Japanese forces invade the Aleutian Islands (the first invasion of American soil in 128 years).
- June 8 – WWII: Attack on Sydney Harbour: The Australian cities of Sydney and Newcastle are shelled by Japanese submarines. The eastern suburbs of both cities are damaged and the east coast is blacked out.
- June 9 – WWII:
  - Nazis burn the Czech village of Lidice in reprisal for the killing of Reinhard Heydrich.
  - (12:30 a.m.) – B-17 Flying Fortress air crash near Auckland.
- June 10 – WWII: The Gestapo massacres 173 male residents of Lidice, Czechoslovakia in retaliation for the killing of Reinhard Heydrich.
- June 12 – The Holocaust: On her 13th birthday, Anne Frank makes the first entry in her new diary.
- June 13 – WWII: The United States opens its Office of War Information, a propaganda center.
- June 18 – WWII: The SS surrounds the church where Jan Kubiš and Jozef Gabčík, the assassins of Reinhard Heydrich, are hiding. Kubiš is fatally wounded in the ensuing shootout and Gabčík commits suicide to avoid capture.
- June 29 – WWII: The Germans launch Case Blue, Army Group South's drive to Stalingrad and the Baku Oil fields.
- June 29 – WWII: The German Eleventh Army under Erich von Manstein takes Sevastopol, although fighting rages until July 9.

July

- July 1–July 27 – WWII: The First Battle of El Alamein.
- July 3 – WWII: Guadalcanal, occupied only by aborigines falls to the Japanese Naval construction force deployed to construct an air field on the island.
- July 4 – WWII in the European Theater of Operations:
  - Twenty-four ships are sunk by German bombers and submarines after Convoy PQ 17 to the Soviet Union is

scattered in the Arctic Ocean to evade the German battleship Tirpitz.
- o US Eighth Air Force inauspiciously flies its first mission in Europe using borrowed British planes and bombs targets in the Netherlands, such as De Kooy airfield attached to Den Helder naval base. Three of six aircraft return; Captain Charles C. Kegelman is the first member of 8th Airforce to be awarded DFC for this mission.
- July 6 – The Holocaust: Anne Frank's family goes into hiding in an attic above her father's office in an Amsterdam warehouse.
- July 8 – Turkish prime minister Refik Saydam died while working in office. For one day he is succeeded by Ahmet Fikri Tüzer
- July 9 – Şükrü Saracoğlu forms the new (13th) government in Turkey.
- July 13 – WWII: U-boats sink 3 more merchant ships in the Gulf of St. Lawrence.
- July 14 – WWII: Germany introduces the Ostvolk Medal for Soviet personnel in the Wehrmacht.
- July 16
  - o The Holocaust: By order of the Vichy France government headed by Pierre Laval, French police officers round-up 13,000–20,000 Jews and imprison them in the Winter Velodrome.
  - o Georges Bégué and others escape from the Mauzac prison camp.
- July 18 – WWII: The Germans test fly the Messerschmitt Me 262 (using only its jets) for the first time.
- July 19 – WWII: Battle of the Atlantic: German Grand Admiral Karl Dönitz orders the last U-boats to withdraw from their United States Atlantic coast positions, in response to an effective American convoy system.
- July 21 – The Japanese establish a beachhead on the north coast of New Guinea in the Buna-Gona area; a small Australian force begins a rearguard action on the Kokoda Track campaign.

- July 22 – The Holocaust: The systematic deportation of Jews from the Warsaw Ghetto begins.
- July 23 – Holocaust: The gas chambers at Treblinka extermination camp begin operation, killing 6,500 Jews newly arrived from the Warsaw Ghetto.
- July 29 – The Presidium of the Supreme Soviet of the USSR institutes the Order of Suvorov, the Order of Kutuzov, and reinstates the Order of Alexander Nevsky.
- July 30
  - WAVES (Women Accepted for Volunteer Emergency Service) in the United States.
  - SS *Robert E. Lee* sunk in the Gulf of Mexico by *U-166* which is itself sunk by the escorting patrol craft.
- July 31 – The Oxford Committee for Famine Relief (Oxfam) is founded in England.

August

- August 7 – WWII: Guadalcanal Campaign begins – The U.S. Navy and the U.S. Marine Corps begin the first American offensive of the war with an amphibious landing on the island of Guadalcanal in the Solomon Islands.
- August 8
  - WWII: Convoy SC 94 loses ten ships as the first to be heavily attacked by U-boats resuming mid-Atlantic wolf pack attacks through the climactic winter of 1942\43.
  - WWII: In Washington, D.C., six German saboteurs are executed for their role in a failed mission of Operation Pastorius. (Two others are cooperative and receive sentences of life imprisonment instead, being freed a few years after the end of the war.)
  - Walt Disney's fifth animated feature film *Bambi* receives its world première in London.

- August 9
    - Indian leader, Mohandas Gandhi is arrested in Bombay by British forces.
    - *Start*, led by the goalkeeper Nikolai Trusevich, play football against the German Luftwaffe team Flakelf in Nazi-occupied Kiev. Against all odds, they win 5–3. Eight of them are later arrested and tortured, and at least four are killed.
    - Leningrad première of Shostakovich's Symphony No. 7 with the city still under siege.
- August 13
    - Quit India resolution is passed by the Bombay session of the All India Congress Committee (AICC), which leads to the start of a historical civil disobedience movement across India.
- August 14 – A massive burst of cosmic rays is detected by instruments in London.
- August 15 – WWII: The American tanker *Ohio* reaches Malta as part of the convoy of *Operation Pedestal*.
- August 16
    - Polish-Jewish teacher Janusz Korczak follows a group of Jewish children into the Treblinka extermination camp.
    - The U.S. Navy blimp *L-8* (Flight 101) comes ashore near San Francisco, eventually coming down in Daly City (the crew is missing).
- August 17 – WWII: First raid by heavy bombers of U.S. Eighth Air Force against occupied France.
- August 19 – WWII: Dieppe Raid: Allied forces raid Dieppe, France.
- August 20 – Plutonium is isolated for the first time at the Metallurgical Laboratory of the University of Chicago.
- August 22 – WWII: Brazil declares war on Germany and Italy.
- August 23 – WWII: Battle of Stalingrad begins: German troops reach the suburbs of Stalingrad.

- August 24 – WWII:
  - Charge of the Savoia Cavalleria at Isbuscenskij: An Italian cavalry regiment attacks Soviet forces with drawn sabres at Isbuscenskij in Russia, one of the last major cavalry charges.
  - North Atlantic convoy ON 122 is attacked by U-boats sinking four ships.
- August 25
  - WWII: Japanese marines land at Milne Bay.
  - Prince George, Duke of Kent, brother to King George VI and King Edward VIII, dies in a flying accident over Morven in Scotland at the age of 39.
- August 30 – Luxembourg is formally annexed to the German Reich.
- August 31 – A general strike is launched in Luxembourg to protest against forced conscription.
- August 31–September 5 – WWII: Battle of Alam el Halfa.

September

- September 2 – The island of Les Casquets in the Channel Islands is raided by the forerunner of the British SAS, the SSRF, led by Major Gus March-Phillipps; this is one of the first raids by Anders Lassen VC. In the raid the entire garrison of 7 is abducted and returned to England as prisoners and the radio and lighthouse wrecked.
- September 3 – The Holocaust: A German attempt to liquidate the Jewish Łachwa Ghetto in occupied Poland leads to an uprising, probably the first ghetto uprising of the war.
- September 5
  - WWII: Battle of Milne Bay: Japanese forces suffer their first defeat on land.
  - The Holocaust: The Jews of Wolbrom in occupied Poland are rounded up by the Germans and their Ukrainian collaborators. What was once a flourishing community suddenly ceases to exist.

- September 9 – WWII: A Japanese floatplane drops incendiary devices at Mount Emily, near Brookings, Oregon, in the first of two "Lookout Air Raids", the first bombing of the continental United States.
- September 10
  - WWII: North Atlantic convoy ON 127 is attacked by U-boats sinking six ships.
  - Women's Auxiliary Ferrying Squadron (WAFS) begins operation in the United States.
- September 12 – The RMS *Laconia*, carrying civilians, Allied soldiers and Italian Prisoners of War, is torpedoed off the coast of West Africa and sinks.
- September 15 – Women's Flying Training Detachment (WFTD) established in the United States.
- September 24 – WWII: Andrée Borrel and Lise de Baissac become the first female SOE agents to be parachuted into occupied France.
- September 27 – WWII: Both commerce raiding German auxiliary cruiser *Stier* and American Liberty ship SS *Stephen Hopkins* sink following a gun battle in the South Atlantic. *Hilfskreuzer Stier* is the only commerce raider to be sunk by a defensively equipped merchant ship.

October

- October 2 – The British cruiser HMS *Curacoa* collides with the liner RMS *Queen Mary* (carrying troops from the United States) off the coast of Donegal and sinks; 338 drown.
- October 3 – The first A-4 rocket is successfully launched from Test Stand VII at Peenemünde, Germany. The rocket flies 147 kilometres wide and reaches a height of 84.5 kilometres, becoming the first man-made object to reach space.
- October 9 – The Statute of Westminster Adoption Act passed by the Parliament of Australia formalizes Australian autonomy from the United Kingdom.

- October 11 – WWII – Battle of Cape Esperance: On the northwest coast of Guadalcanal, United States Navy ships intercept and defeat a Japanese fleet on their way to reinforce troops on the island.
- October 13 – WWII: North Atlantic convoy SC 104 is attacked by U-boats sinking seven ships.
- October 14 – A U-boat sinks the ferry SS *Caribou* off Newfoundland, killing 137.
- October 16
  - A hurricane and flood in Bombay kill 40,000.
  - *The Mouse of Tomorrow* featuring the debut of Mighty Mouse is released.
- October 18 – WWII – Hitler issues Commando Order which stipulates that all Allied commandos encountered by German forces should be executed immediately without trial, even in proper uniforms, in response to the Dieppe Raid and Operation Basalt conducted by the Allies. After the war, the Nuremberg trials found this order a direct violation of the laws and customs of war.
- October 21 – A Royal New Zealand Air Force Torpedo Bomber sinks the German MS Palatia (1928) with a loss of 946 people.
- October 23 – Award-winning composer and Hollywood songwriter Ralph Rainger ("Thanks for the Memory") is among 12 people killed in the mid-air collision between an American Airlines DC-3 airliner and a U.S. Army bomber near Palm Springs, California.
- October 23–November 4 – WWII: Second Battle of El Alamein: British troops go on the offensive against the Axis forces.
- October 26 – WWII: Battle of the Santa Cruz Islands: Two Japanese aircraft carriers are heavily damaged and one U.S. Navy carrier is sunk.
- October 28 – The Alaska Highway is completed.
- October 29 – The Holocaust: In the United Kingdom, leading clergymen and political figures hold a public meeting to register outrage over Nazi Germany's persecution of Jews.
- October 30 – WWII:

- o U-boats sink eleven ships attacking diversionary convoy SL 125, but move out of the path of approaching troopships carrying Allied Operation Torch invasion forces.
- o British sailors board *U-559* as it sinks in the Mediterranean and retrieve its Enigma machine and codebooks.

November

- November 1 – WWII: North Atlantic convoy SC 107 is heavily attacked by U-boats sinking fifteen ships.
- November 2 – A USAAF squadron, including B-24 Liberators, intercepts many Luftwaffe patrols off the coast of Oran, Algeria.
- November 3 – WWII: Second Battle of El Alamein: German forces under Erwin Rommel are forced to retreat during the night.
- November 8 – WWII:
  - o Operation Torch: United States and United Kingdom forces land in French North Africa.
  - o French Resistance Coup in Algiers: 400 French civil resisters neutralize the Vichyist XIXth Army Corps and the Vichyist generals (Juin, Darlan, etc.) thus allowing the immediate success of Operation Torch in Algiers, and ultimately the whole of French North Africa.
- November 9 – WWII: U.S serviceman Edward Leonski is hanged at Melbourne's Pentridge Prison for the "Brown-Out" murders of three women in May.
- November 10 – WWII: In violation of a 1940 armistice, Germany invades Vichy France, following French Admiral François Darlan's agreement to an armistice with the Allies in North Africa.
- November 12 – WWII: Guadalcanal Campaign: A naval battle near Guadalcanal starts between Japanese and American forces.
- November 13 – WWII:
  - o Guadalcanal Campaign: Aviators from the USS *Enterprise* sink the Japanese battleship *Hiei*.
  - o British forces capture Tobruk.
  - o

- November 15 – WWII:
  - The Naval Battle of Guadalcanal ends: Although the United States Navy suffers heavy losses, it retains control of Guadalcanal.
  - A BOAC scheduled passenger flight, a DC-3 with registration G-AGBB, (formerly KLM PH-ALI, Ibis), en route between Lisbon and Bristol, is attacked over the Bay of Biscay by German fighters. Although damaged, it escapes and lands in England. Other attacks follow on the same aircraft and scheduled route: April 19 and June 1, 1943 (fatal).
  - British forces capture Derna, Libya.
- November 18 – WWII: North Atlantic convoy ON 144 is attacked by U-boats sinking five ships.
- November 19 – WWII: Battle of Stalingrad: Soviet Union forces under General Georgy Zhukov launch the Operation Uranus counter-attacks at Stalingrad, turning the tide of the battle in the USSR's favor.
- November 20 – WWII: British forces capture Benghazi.
- November 21 – The completion of the Alaska Highway (also known as the Alcan Highway) is celebrated (however, the "highway" is not usable by general vehicles until 1943).
- November 22 – WWII: Battle of Stalingrad: The situation for the German attackers of Stalingrad seems desperate during the Soviet counter-attack Operation Uranus, and General Friedrich Paulus sends Adolf Hitler a telegram saying that the German Sixth Army is surrounded.
- November 23 – WWII
  - A U-boat sinks the SS *Ben Lomond* off the coast of Brazil. One crewman, Chinese second steward Poon Lim, is separated from the others and spends 130 days adrift until he is rescued on April 3, 1943.
  - Legislation approves the United States Coast Guard Women's Reserve to help fill jobs and free men to serve during the war

effort. They are known as the SPARS ("Semper Paratus, Always Ready!")

- November 25–26 – WWII: Operation Harling: A British Special Operations Executive team, together with Greek Resistance fighters, blows up the Gorgopotamos viaduct in the first major sabotage act in occupied continental Europe.
- November 26 – The movie *Casablanca* premières at the Hollywood Theater in New York City.
- November 27 – WWII: At Toulon, the French navy scuttles its ships and submarines to keep them out of Nazi hands.
- November 28
  - Cocoanut Grove fire: A fire in the Cocoanut Grove night club in Boston, Massachusetts, kills 491.
  - The large-scale German "pacification" of the Zamojszczyzna region of Poland begins.
- November 29 – The Blue Star Line cargo liner MV *Dunedin Star* runs aground on the Skeleton Coast of Namibia. Crew and passengers survive following a 26-day overland trek to Windhoek.
- November 30 – WWII: Battle of Tassafaronga – In a nighttime naval battle as part of the Guadalcanal Campaign, ships of the Imperial Japanese Navy defeat those of the United States Navy.

December

- December 1 – Gasoline rationing begins in the United States.
- December 2 – Manhattan Project: Below the bleachers of Stagg Field at the University of Chicago, a team led by Enrico Fermi initiates the first self-sustaining nuclear chain reaction (a coded message, "The Italian navigator has landed in the new world" is then sent to U.S. President Franklin D. Roosevelt).
- December 4
  - The Holocaust: In Warsaw, two women, Zofia Kossak and Wanda Filipowicz, risk their lives by setting up the Council for the Assistance of the Jews.
  - WWII: USAAF bombers make their first raid on Italy.

- December 7 – WWII: British commandos conduct Operation Frankton, a raid on shipping in Bordeaux harbour.
- December 8 – A fire at Seacliff Lunatic Asylum in New Zealand kills 39 patients.
- December 17 – The Allies issue the Joint Declaration by Members of the United Nations, the first time they publicly acknowledge the Holocaust.
- December 22
  - An avalanche in Aliquippa, Pennsylvania kills 26, including Vulcan Crucible Steel heir-apparent Samuel A. Stafford Sr., when two 100 ton boulders fall on a bus filled with wartime steel workers on their way home.
  - An airplane carrying prominent Ustashe general Jure Francetić crashes. Francetić dies as result of the injuries on December 27.
- December 24 – French Admiral Darlan, the former Vichy leader who has switched over to the Allies following the Torch landings, is assassinated in Algiers.
- December 27 – The Union of Pioneers of Yugoslavia is founded.
- December 28 – North Atlantic Convoy ON 154 is heavily attacked by U-boats sinking thirteen ships.

Date unknown

- DDT is first used as a pesticide.
- 1942 FIFA World Cup competition in Association football, which Nazi Germany sought to host, is not held, due to World War II.

Births

January

Stephen Hawking

Muhammad Ali

Eusébio

- January 1
  - Country Joe McDonald, American musician
  - Gennadi Sarafanov, Russian cosmonaut (d. 2005)
  -

- January 2
  - Dennis Hastert, American politician, Speaker of the United States House of Representatives
  - Hugh Shelton, American military leader, Chairman of the Joint Chiefs of Staff
- January 3
  - László Sólyom, President of Hungary
  - John Thaw, English actor (d. 2002)
- January 4
  - Bolaji Akinyemi, Nigerian professor of political science
  - Dame Marcela Contreras, Chilean-British immunologist and educator
- January 5
  - Maurizio Pollini, Italian pianist
  - Charlie Rose, American television anchor, talk show host
- January 7 – Vasily Alekseyev, Soviet weightlifter
- January 8
  - Stephen Hawking, British physicist
  - Junichiro Koizumi, 56th Prime Minister of Japan
- January 14 – Yogesh Kumar Sabharwal, Chief Justice of India
- January 16 – René Angélil, Canadian singer and manager (d. 2016)
- January 17
  - Muhammad Ali, American boxer (d. 2016)
  - Ulf Hoelscher, German violinist
- January 19 – Michael Crawford, English actor, singer and entertainer
- January 25
  - Carl Eller, American football player
  - Eusébio, Mozambican Portuguese footballer (d. 2014)
- January 26 – Soad Hosny, Egyptian actress (d. 2001)
- January 28
  - Hans Jürgen Bäumler, German figure skater, actor, pop singer and television host
  - Erkki Pohjanheimo, Finnish TV-producer and director
  -

- January 31
  - Daniela Bianchi, Italian actress
  - Derek Jarman, English director and writer (d. 1994)

February

Terry Jones

Ehud Barak

Brian Jones

- February 1
  - Bibi Besch, Austrian-American actress (d. 1996)

- Terry Jones, Welsh actor and writer
- February 2 – Graham Nash, English rock musician (The Hollies)
- February 5 – Roger Staubach, American football player
- February 6 – Ahmad-Jabir Ahmadov Ismail oghlu, Azeri professor and academic
- February 7 – Gareth Hunt, English actor (d. 2007)
- February 9 – Carole King, American singer and composer
- February 10 – Howard Mudd, American offensive lineman & offensive line coach
- February 12 – Ehud Barak, Prime Minister of Israel
- February 13
  - Carol Lynley, American actress
  - Donald E. Williams, American astronaut (d. 2016)
  - Peter Tork, American musician, performer
- February 14 – Michael Bloomberg, American businessman, philanthropist, and the founder of Bloomberg L.P., Mayor of New York City
- February 15 – Sherry Jackson, American actress
- February 19 – Paul Krause, American football player
- February 20
  - Phil Esposito, Canadian hockey player
  - Mitch McConnell, United States Senator (R-KY)
- February 21 – Margarethe von Trotta, German actress, film director, and writer
- February 24 – Joseph Lieberman, American politician
- February 25 – Karen Grassle, American actress
- February 27
  - Michel Forget, Canadian actor
  - Robert H. Grubbs, American chemist, Nobel Prize laureate
- February 28
  - Brian Jones, English musician (The Rolling Stones) (d. 1969)
  - Dino Zoff, Italian footballer and manager

March

Ali Abdullah Saleh

Aretha Franklin

Daniel Dennett

- March 2
  - John Irving, American author
  - Lou Reed, American singer-songwriter and guitarist (d. 2013)
- March 5 – Felipe González, Prime Minister of Spain
- March 7
  - Tammy Faye Bakker, American evangelist, singer and television personality (d. 2007)

- o Michael Eisner, American film studio executive
- March 9
  - o Pedro Bandeira, Brazilian children's author
  - o John Cale, Welsh composer and musician
- March 12
  - o Ratko Mladić, former Bosnian Serb military leader
  - o Jimmy Wynn, American baseball player
- March 13
  - o Dave Cutler, American software engineer
  - o Scatman John, American musician (d. 1999)
  - o George Negus, Australian author, journalist, and television presenter
- March 16 – James Soong, Taiwan politician
- March 21 – Ali Abdullah Saleh, President of Yemen (1990 to 2012)
- March 23 – Walter Rodney, Guyanese historian and political figure
- March 25 – Aretha Franklin, American singer
- March 26 – Erica Jong, American author
- March 27
  - o John E. Sulston, British chemist; recipient of the Nobel Prize in Physiology or Medicine
  - o Michael York, English actor
- March 28
  - o Neil Kinnock, British Labour leader
  - o Mike Newell, British film director
  - o Conrad Schumann, East German border guard (d. 1998)
  - o Jerry Sloan, American basketball coach
  - o Daniel Dennett, American philosopher
- March 29
  - o Scott Wilson, American actor
  - o Kenichi Ogata, Japanese voice actor
- March 30 – Ruben Kun, Nauruan politician and former President of Nauru

April

Barbra Streisand

- April 1 – Samuel R. Delany, American science fiction author
- April 2
  - Leon Russell, American singer, songwriter, pianist, and guitarist
  - Hiroyuki Sakai, Japanese chef
  - Roshan Seth, British actor
  - Yury Yarov, Russian politician and a former deputy prime minister
- April 3 – Marsha Mason, American actress
- April 5
  - Pascal Couchepin, Swiss Federal Councilor
  - Peter Greenaway, Welsh filmmaker
- April 6 – Barry Levinson, American film producer and director
- April 8 – Roger Chapman, British rock singer (Family)
- April 9 – James Cowan, Australian novelist
- April 10
  - Hayedeh, Iranian singer (d. 1990)
  - Nick Auf der Maur, Canadian journalist and politician (d. 1998)
- April 12
  - Jacob Zuma, President of South Africa
  - Carlos Alberto Reutemann, Argentine racing driver and politician
  -

- April 14
  - Valeriy Brumel, Russian athlete (d. 2003)
  - Valentin Lebedev, Russian cosmonaut
- April 15
  - Kenneth Lay, American businessman (d. 2006)
  - Julie Sommars, American actress
- April 17
  - Kenas Aroi, Nauruan politician
  - Buster Williams, American jazz bassist
- April 19 – Frank Elstner, German television presenter
- April 20 – Arto Paasilinna, Finnish author
- April 23 – Sandra Dee, American actress (d. 2005)
  - Christian Frémont, French politician (d. 2014)
- April 24 – Barbra Streisand, American singer, actress, composer
- April 25
  - Katsuji Adachi, Japanese professional wrestler
  - Jon Kyl, American politician; United States Senator (R-AZ)
- April 26
  - Claudine Auger, French actress
  - Michael Kergin, Canadian diplomat
  - Bobby Rydell, American singer
- April 27
  - Ruth Glick, American writer
  - Jim Keltner, American drummer

May

Ian Dury

- May 2 – Jacques Rogge, Belgian International Olympic Committee president
- May 3 – Věra Čáslavská, Czech gymnast
- May 5 – Tammy Wynette, American country singer (d. 1998)
- May 8 – Terry Neill, Northern Irish footballer and football manager
- May 9 – John Ashcroft, United States Attorney General
- May 10 – Youssouf Sambo Bâ, Burkinabé politician
- May 12 – Ian Dury, British musician (d. 2000)
- May 17 – Taj Mahal, American singer and guitarist
- May 22
  - Barbara Parkins, Canadian actress
  - Rich Garcia, American Major League Baseball Umpire
- May 23 – Gabriel Liiceanu, Romanian philosopher
- May 24 – Ichirō Ozawa, Japanese politician
- May 28
  - Stanley B. Prusiner, American scientist, recipient of the Nobel Prize in Physiology or Medicine
  - James Tien, Hong Kong-Taiwanese actor
- May 31 – Jahar Dasgupta, Indian painter

June

Teodoro Obiang Nguema Mbasogo

Roger Ebert

Paul McCartney

Brian Wilson

- June 2 – Eduard Malofeyev, Russian football coach and former international player
- June 3 – Curtis Mayfield, American musician (d. 1999)
- June 5 – Teodoro Obiang Nguema Mbasogo, President of Equatorial Guinea and Chairperson of the African Union
- June 6 – Klaus Bednarz, German journalist and writer (d. 2015)
- June 10
  - Gordon Burns, British journalist and TV presenter
  - Preston Manning, Canadian politician
- June 11 – Jeannette Vivian Corbiere Lavell, Canadian-Anishinaabe activist

- June 11 – Jack Hales meteorologist in the government for 44 years
- June 12 – Bert Sakmann, German physiologist, Nobel Prize laureate
- June 14 – Abdulsalami Abubakar, former President of Nigeria
- June 16 – John Rostill, English bassist, musician and composer (The Shadows) (d. 1973)
- June 17 – Mohamed ElBaradei, Egyptian International Atomic Energy Agency director, recipient of the Nobel Peace Prize
- June 18
  - Roger Ebert, American film critic and television personality (d. 2013)
  - Thabo Mbeki, President of South Africa and politician
  - Paul McCartney, British musician and composer (The Beatles)
  - Nick Tate, Australian actor
  - Hans Vonk, Dutch conductor (d. 2004)
- June 20 – Brian Wilson, American singer-composer-producer (The Beach Boys)
- June 24 – Michele Lee, American actress and singer
- June 26
  - James J. Dillon, American professional wrestling manager
  - Gilberto Gil, Brazilian singer, politician
  - June 28 – Rupert Sheldrake, British biochemist

July

Vicente Fox

Harrison Ford

- July 1
  - Geneviève Bujold, French-Canadian actress
  - Andraé Crouch, American gospel singer (d. 2015)
- July 2 – Vicente Fox, President of Mexico
- July 4
  - Floyd Little, American football player
  - Prince Michael of Kent
- July 5 – Hannes Löhr, German footballer (d. 2016)
- July 7 – Carmen Duncan, Australian actress
- July 9 – Richard Roundtree, American actor
- July 10
  - Ronnie James Dio, American singer (d. 2010)
  - Pyotr Klimuk, Russian cosmonaut
- July 13
  - Harrison Ford, American actor
  - Roger McGuinn, American musician (The Byrds)
- July 14 – Javier Solana, Spanish politician and diplomat
- July 15 – Mil Máscaras, Mexican professional wrestler
- July 16 – Margaret Court, Australian tennis player
- July 18 – Adolf Ogi, member of the Swiss Federal Council
- July 23 – Myra Hindley, English multiple murderer (d. 2002)
- July 24 – Chris Sarandon, American actor
- July 26 – Hannelore Elsner, German actress

- July 27 – Dennis Ralston, American tennis player
- July 28 – Kaari Utrio, Finnish writer

August

Isabel Allende

José Eduardo dos Santos

- August 1
  - Jerry Garcia, American musician (d. 1995)
  - Giancarlo Giannini, Italian actor
- August 2 – Isabel Allende, Chilean writer
- August 4 – David Lange, Prime Minister of New Zealand (d. 2005)
- August 6 – Evelyn Hamann, German actress (d. 2007)
- August 7
  - Tobin Bell, American film and television actor
  - Garrison Keillor, American writer and radio host; Prairie Home Companion

- August 13 – Arthur K. Cebrowski, American admiral (d. 2005)
- August 15 – Friede Springer, German publisher and widow of Axel Springer
- August 18 – Judith Keppel, first person to win £1,000,000 on *Who Wants to Be a Millionaire?* (in the UK)
- August 19 – Fred Thompson, American politician and actor (d. 2015)
- August 20 – Isaac Hayes, American singer and actor (d. 2008)
- August 24 – Hans Peter Korff, German actor
- August 27 – "Captain" Daryl Dragon, American musician (Captain & Tennille)
- August 28 – José Eduardo dos Santos, President of Angola
- August 31 – Isao Aoki, Japanese golfer

September

- September 3
  - Michael Hui, Hong Kong film comedian
  - Al Jardine, American musician (The Beach Boys)
- September 5
  - Björn Haugan, Norwegian operatic lyric tenor (d. 2009)
  - Werner Herzog, German filmmaker
- September 7 – Alan Haskvitz, American educator
- September 8 – Želimir Žilnik, Serbian film director
- September 13 – Hissène Habré, President of Chad
- September 14 – Bernard MacLaverty, Irish writer
- September 15 – Wen Jiabao, Premier of the People's Republic of China
- September 16 – Tadamasa Goto, Japanese yakuza boss
- September 17 – Des Lynam, British television host, presenter
- September 18
  - Gabriella Ferri, Italian singer
  - Wolfgang Schäuble, German politician
- September 19 – Freda Payne, American singer and actress

- September 20 – Rose Francine Rogombé, Gabonese lawyer and politician (d. 2015)
- September 22
  - Wu Ma, Chinese film actor, director, producer and writer
  - Marlena Shaw, American jazz singer
  - David Stern, American commissioner of the National Basketball Association
- September 24 – Ilkka "Danny" Lipsanen, Finnish singer
- September 29
  - Madeline Kahn, American actress (d. 1999)
  - Ian McShane, English actor
  - Jean-Luc Ponty, French jazz violinist
- September 30 – Frankie Lymon, American singer (d. 1968)

October

Amitabh Bachchan

Bob Hoskins

- October 1 – Günter Wallraff, German investigative journalist
- October 2 – Asha Parekh, Indian actress
- October 3
  - Earl Hindman, American actor (d. 2003)

- o Roberto Perfumo, Argentine footballer and sports commentator (d. 2016)
- October 6
  - o Britt Ekland, Swedish actress
  - o Fred Travalena, American comedian and impressionist (d. 2009)
- October 7
  - o Ronald Baecker, American computer scientist
  - o Joy Behar, American comedian and television personality
- October 8 – Stanley Bates, British actor and screenwriter
- October 11 – Amitabh Bachchan, Indian actor
- October 12 – Daliah Lavi, Israeli actress and singer
- October 13
  - o Rutanya Alda, Latvian-American actress
  - o Jerry Jones, American football team owner
- October 14 – Evelio Javier, Filipino politician, lawyer, and civil servant (d. 1986)
- October 19 – Andrew Vachss, American author and attorney
- October 20 – Christiane Nüsslein-Volhard, German biologist, recipient of the Nobel Prize in Physiology or Medicine
- October 21 – Judith Sheindlin, American retired judge turned television personality (*Judge Judy*)
- October 23 – Michael Crichton, American author (d. 2008)
- October 24 – Frank Delaney, Irish novelist, journalist and broadcaster
- October 26 – Bob Hoskins, British actor (d. 2014)
- October 29 – Bob Ross, American painter and television presenter (d. 1995)
- October 31 – David Ogden Stiers, American actor and voice-over artist

November

Martin Scorsese

Joe Biden

Jimi Hendrix

Billy Connolly

- November 1
  - Larry Flynt, American publisher (*Hustler*)
  - Ralph Klein, Canadian politician (d. 2013)
  - Marcia Wallace, American actress and comedian (d. 2013)
- November 2
  - Shere Hite, American-born German sexologist
  - Stefanie Powers, American actress
- November 5 – Pierangelo Bertoli, Italian singer-songwriter (d. 2002)
- November 6 – Jean Shrimpton, English model and actress
- November 7 – Tom Peters, American writer
- November 8
  - Angel Cordero, Jr., Puerto Rican jockey
  - Fernando Sorrentino, Argentine writer
- November 10
  - Robert F. Engle, American economist, Nobel Prize laureate
  - Hans-Rudolf Merz, Swiss federal councillor
- November 15 – Daniel Barenboim, Argentine-born pianist and conductor
- November 16 – Joanna Pettet, British-born Canadian actress
- November 17
  - Derek Clayton, Australian long-distance runner
  - Bob Gaudio, American musician
  - Kang Kek Iew, Cambodian politician and criminal
  - István Rosztóczy, Hungarian microbiologist

- o Martin Scorsese, American film director
- November 18
  - o Linda Evans, American soap actress
  - o Susan Sullivan, American soap actress
- November 20 – Joe Biden, 47th Vice President of the United States
- November 22
  - o Francis K. Butagira, Ugandan ambassador
  - o Dick Stockton, American sports announcer
- November 24 – Billy Connolly, Scottish comedian and singer
- November 25 – Rosa von Praunheim, German film director, author and painter
- November 26 – Khalil Kalfat, Egyptian intellectual and writer
- November 27
  - o Manolo Blahnik, Spanish shoe designer
  - o Jimi Hendrix, American guitarist (d. 1970)
- November 28 – Paul Warfield, American football player
- November 29 – Philippe Huttenlocher, Swiss baritone
- November 30 – André Brahic, French astrophysicist (d. 2016)

December

Muhammadu Buhari

Hu Jintao

- December 3 – Alice Schwarzer, German feminist, founder and publisher of the German feminist journal EMMA
- December 4 – Gemma Jones, British actress
- December 6 – Peter Handke, Austrian novelist
- December 7
  - Reginald Lewis, American Businessman (d. 1993)
  - Peter Tomarken, American game-show host (d. 2006)
- December 9 – Dick Butkus, American football player
- December 12 – Peter Sarstedt, British musician
- December 17
  - Muhammadu Buhari, Nigerian president
  - Paul Butterfield, American musician (d. 1987)
- December 20 – Bob Hayes, American athlete
- December 21
  - Hu Jintao, General Secretary of the Communist Party of China, President of the People's Republic of China
  - Carla Thomas, American singer
- December 27 – Thomas Menino, 53rd Mayor of Boston, Massachusetts (d. 2014)
- December 29 – Rajesh Khanna, Indian actor (d. 2012)
- December 30
  - Betty Aberlin, American actress
  - Allan Gotthelf, American philosopher (d. 2013)
  - Michael Nesmith, American singer-songwriter, performer
  - Janko Prunk, Slovenian historian

Date unknown

- Muammar Gaddafi, former leader of Libya (d. 2011) — believed to have been born in 1942

Deaths

January

Carole Lombard

- January 4
  - Mel Sheppard, American athlete (b. 1883)
  - Otis Skinner, American stage and film actor (b. 1858)
- January 6 – Henri de Baillet-Latour, Belgian International Olympic Committee president (b. 1876)
- January 9 – Heber Doust Curtis, American astronomer (b. 1872)
- January 14 – Porfirio Barba-Jacob, Colombian poet and writer (b. 1883)
- January 16
  - Prince Arthur, Duke of Connaught and Strathearn, second youngest son of Queen Victoria (b. 1850)
  - Carole Lombard, American actress (air crash) (b. 1908)
- January 18 – James P. Parker, United States Navy commodore (b. 1855)
- January 22 – Walter Sickert, English Impressionist painter (b. 1860)
- January 23 – Nazareno Strampelli, talian agronomist and plant breeder (b. 1866)
- January 26 – Felix Hausdorff, German mathematician (suicide) (b. 1868)

February

- February 8 – Fritz Todt, Nazi German engineer (b. 1891)
- February 9 – Lauri Kristian Relander, 2nd President of Finland (b. 1883)
- February 11 – Ugo Pasquale Mifsud, 3rd Prime Minister of Malta (b. 1889)
- February 12 – Grant Wood, American painter (b. 1891)
- February 13 – Epitácio Pessoa, former president of Brazil (b. 1865)
- February 14 – Mirosław Ferić, Polish pilot of the No. 303 Squadron in Northolt (b. 1915)
- February 19 – Frank Abbandando, American gangster (executed) (b. 1910)
- February 20 – Hamad ibn Isa Al Khalifa, ruler of Bahrain (b. 1872)
- February 22 – Stefan Zweig, Austrian writer (suicide with wife) (b. 1881)
- February 28 – Karel Doorman, Dutch admiral (killed in action) (b. 1889)

March

Robert Bosch

William Bragg

- March 1
  - George S. Rentz, United States Navy Chaplain and Navy Cross winner (b. 1882)
  - Cornelius Vanderbilt III, American military officer, inventor, and engineer (b. 1873)
- March 3 – Prince Amedeo, Duke of Aosta, Italian nobleman and military officer, Viceroy of Italian East Africa (b. 1898)
- March 7 – Pierre Semard, French Communist leader (executed) (b. 1887)
- March 8 – José Raúl Capablanca, Cuban chess player (b. 1888)
- March 12
  - William Henry Bragg, English physicist, Nobel Prize laureate (b. 1862)
  - Robert Bosch, German industrialist, engineer and inventor (b. 1861)
  - Enric Morera i Viura, Spanish composer (b. 1865)
- March 14 – René Bull, British illustrator and photographer (b. 1872)
- March 21 – J. S. Woodsworth, Canadian politician (b. 1874)
- March 23 – Marcelo Torcuato de Alvear, 20th President of Argentina (b. 1868)
- March 27
  - John W. Wilcox, Jr., American admiral (lost overboard) (b. 1882)
  - Julio González, Spanish sculptor and painter (b. 1876)

April

Lucy Maud Montgomery

- April 15
  - Robert Musil, Austrian-born novelist (b. 1880)
  - Joshua Pim, Irish tennis player (b. 1869)
- April 16 – Princess Alexandra of Saxe-Coburg and Gotha, granddaughter of Queen Victoria (b. 1878)
- April 17 – Jean Baptiste Perrin, French physicist, Nobel Prize laureate (b. 1870)
- April 18 – Gertrude Vanderbilt Whitney, American heiress, socialite and sculptor (b. 1875)
- April 24
  - Deenanath Mangeshkar, Indian singer and composer (b. 1900)
  - Lucy Maud Montgomery, Canadian writer (b. 1874)
- April 27 – Arthur L. Bristol, American admiral (b. 1886)

May

John Barrymore

- May 3 – Thorvald Stauning, Prime Minister of Denmark (b. 1873)
- May 7
  - José Abad Santos, Filipino chief justice of the Supreme Court (b. 1886)
  - Felix Weingartner, Yugoslavian conductor (b. 1863)
- May 9 – Graham McNamee, American radio announcer (b. 1888)
- May 10 – Joe Weber, American vaudevillian (b. 1867)
- May 14 – Frank Churchill, American composer (b. 1901)
- May 16 – Bronisław Malinowski, Polish anthropologist (b. 1884)
- May 19 – A. E. Waite, British occultist (b. 1857)
- May 27 – Chen Duxiu, General Secretary of the Communist Party of China (b. 1879)
- May 29
  - John Barrymore, American actor (b. 1882)
  - Akiko Yosano, Japanese author, poet (b. 1878)

June

- June 4
  - Lofton R. Henderson, United States Marine Corps aviator and commanding officer of Marine Scout Bomber Squadron 241 (VMSB-241); killed in action at the Battle of Midway (b. 1903)
  - Reinhard Heydrich, headed the Nazi Reich Main Security Office and was Reich governor of Bohemia and Moravia (b. 1904)
  - John C. Waldron, United States Navy aviator and commander of Torpedo Squadron 8, killed in action at the Battle of Midway (b. 1900)
  - Tamon Yamaguchi, Japanese admiral, killed in action at the Battle of Midway (b. 1892)
- June 5 – Virginia Lee Corbin, American actress (b. 1910)
- June 7 – Alan Blumlein, English electronics engineer (b. 1903)
- June 25 – Zénon Bernard, Luxembourgish communist politician (b. 1893)

- June 26 – Gene Stack, first American major league baseball player to be drafted during World War II as well as the first to die in service (b. 1920)
- June 30 – William Henry Jackson, American photographer (b. 1843)

July

- July 1 – Peadar Toner Mac Fhionnlaoich, Irish-language writer (b. 1857)
- July 8
  - Louis Franchet d'Espèrey, French general (b. 1856)
  - Refik Saydam, prime minister of Turkey in his office (b. 1881)
- July 15 – Wenceslao Vinzons, Filipino politician and resistance leader (bayoneted to death) (b. 1910)
- July 18 – George Sutherland, English-born American Supreme Court Justice (b. 1862)
- July 23 – Adam Czerniaków, Polish engineer and senator (suicide) (b. 1880)
- July 24 – Roberto María Ortiz, 24th President of Argentina (b. 1886)
- July 26 – Roberto Arlt, Argentine writer (b. 1900)
- July 28 – Flinders Petrie, English Egyptologist (b. 1853)
- July 29 – Louis Borno, 28th President of Haiti (b. 1865)
- July 30 – Jimmy Blanton, American bassist (b. 1918)

August

Richard Willstätter

- August 3
  - James Cruze, American actor and director (b. 1884)
  - Richard Willstätter, German chemist, Nobel Prize laureate (b. 1872)
- August 9 – Edith Stein, German philosopher and Catholic saint (assassinated) (b. 1891)
- August 12 – Phillips Holmes, American actor (b. 1907)
- August 21 – Kiyonao Ichiki, Japanese army officer (killed in action) (b. 1892)
- August 22 – Michel Fokine, Russian choreographer and dancer (b. 1880)
- August 25 – Prince George, Duke of Kent, fourth eldest son of George V (b. 1902)
- August 29 – Charles Urban, film producer (b. 1867)

September

- September 14 – Ezra Seymour Gosney, American philanthropist and eugenicist (b. 1855)
- September 30 – Hans-Joachim Marseille, German World War II fighter ace (b. 1919)

October

- October 1 – Ants Piip, 7th Prime Minister and 1st State Elder of Estonia (b. 1884)
- October 6 – Siegmund Glücksmann, German-Jewish politician (b. 1884)
- October 12 – Aritomo Gotō, Japanese admiral (killed in action) (b. 1888)
- October 15 – Dame Marie Tempest, English actress (b. 1864)
- October 20 – May Robson, Australian actress (b. 1858)
- October 23 – Ralph Rainger, American composer and songwriter (b. 1901)
- October 24 – James C. Morton, American character actor (b. 1884)

November

- November 1 – Hugo Distler, German composer (b. 1908)
- November 5 – George M. Cohan, American songwriter and entertainer (b. 1878)
- November 9 – Edna May Oliver, American actress (b. 1883)
- November 12 – Laura Hope Crews, American actress (b. 1879)
- November 13
  - Daniel J. Callaghan, American admiral and Medal of Honor recipient (killed in action) (b. 1890)
  - Norman Scott, American admiral and Medal of Honor recipient (killed in action) (b. 1889)
- November 16 – Joseph Schmidt, Polish tenor (b. 1904)
- November 19 – Bruno Schulz, Polish writer and painter (shot) (b. 1892)
- November 21 – Count Leopold Berchtold, Austro-Hungarian foreign minister (b. 1863)
- November 23
  - Tomitarō Horii, Japanese general (b. 1890)
  - Hernando Siles Reyes, 37th President of Bolivia (b. 1882)
- November 24
  - Guido Masiero, Italian World War I flying ace and aviation pioneer (b. 1895)
  - Francesco Agello, Italian aviator (b. 1902)
- November 30
  - Buck Jones, American actor (b. 1891)
  - Anthony M. Rud, American writer (b. 1893)

December

- December 6 – Amos Rusie, American baseball player and MLB Hall of Famer (b. 1871)
- December 7 – Orland Steen Loomis, Governor-elect of Wisconsin (b. 1893)

- December 12 – Helen Westley, stage and film character actress (b. 1875)
- December 21 – Franz Boas, German anthropologist (b. 1858)
- December 24 – François Darlan, French admiral (assassinated) (b. 1881)
- December 27 – William G. Morgan, inventor of volleyball (b. 1870)
- December 30 – Nevile Henderson, British diplomat (b. 1882)

In the News

War Bonds introduced raising $13 billion.

Voice of America begins broadcasting.

Car Makers switch from making cars to making War Materials.

26 countries agree to create the United nations.

The minimum draft age is lowered from 21 to 18.

Britians asked to bathe in 5 inches of water or less to help the war effort.

Singapore Surrenders to the Japanese.

The classic film "Casablanca" has its premiere.

US Gas Rationing goes into effect 3 gallons per week.

The Battle of Midway begins on June 4th.

In Allied countries around the world government war efforts encourage the population to help by giving scrap metal as much needed raw materials for guns and tanks.

www.ingramcontent.com/pod-product-compliance
Lightning Source LLC
Chambersburg PA
CBHW072017290526

45787CB00013B/1202